PEARL HARBOR STORY

Authentic information and pictures of the

attack on Pearl Harbor

December 7, 1941

by

Captain William T. Rice, USNR (Ret)

Published by Swak, Inc.
P. O. Box 8081, Honolulu, Hawaii
Printed by Tongg Publishing Co., Ltd.
Honolulu, Hawaii, U.S.A.

ELEVENTH PRINTING, 1975

$3.00

CONTENTS

KEWALO BASIN, only two miles Ewa of Waikiki, is home port for many boats. It is a man-made harbor owned and maintained by the State of Hawaii. Here one sees, gently tugging on their mooring lines, commercial cruise boats, commercial fishing boats, and charter boats of the sport-fishing fleet.

It is also the site of Hawaiian Tuna Packers processing and canning plant, which receives its supply of tuna from commercial fishing boats that range far and near on the Pacific Ocean. During the war the local fishing fleet was taken over by the U.S. Government for patrol duty. The Military used the company's shipyard and cold storage plant, and converted the cannery into an aircraft equipment assembly plant.

Fisherman's Wharf, a restaurant with distinctive nautical decor and atmosphere, is located dockside at the foot of Ward Street. Tourist and local patrons alike gather at the restaurant to enjoy its fine seafood specialties and gaze out at the ever-changing activities of Kewalo Basin.

DIAMOND HEAD, sometimes spoken of as the "Gibraltar of the Pacific," is an extinct volcano crater. The name has no connection with any Hawaiian words or legends but came from the finding of some brilliant rocks on its slopes thought to be diamonds by the visitor who found them. The Hawaiian name for the crater is Leahi. Its picturesque profile has been a symbol of Hawaii for many years.

Soon after the Pearl Harbor attack Diamond Head bristled with gun emplacements, barbed wire and defensive Army Units. All of the island's beaches were readied for a second attack or landing of Japanese forces that never appeared.

From Diamond Head to Pearl Harbor is about nine miles on the south shore of Oahu. The two mountain ranges of Oahu are the Waianae Range to the west and the Koolau Range to the east north-east. The major portion of Honolulu is along the south shore and in the valleys of the Koolau Range.

4.

PUNCHBOWL is a flat topped hill at the foot of higher mountains that is only a short distance from downtown Honolulu. It is an extinct volcano crater estimated to be 75,000 years old.

The Hawaiian name is Puowaina, meaning reverence, and legend has referred to the area as a resting place. In contrast to that reverence, there were guns mounted on Punchbowl during the early days of the Monarchy because of the strategic position overlooking Honolulu Harbor.

In 1949 the 112 acres on the floor of the crater were dedicated as the National Memorial of the Pacific. More than 16,000 war casualties are buried here including veterans of the Spanish American War through the crisis in Viet Nam. Ernie Pyle, the well-known correspondent who befriended the GI in World War II, is among them.

The "Garden of the Missing" is a monument in Punchbowl dedicated to men missing in action. Its poignant inscription reads: "The Solemn Pride That Must Be Yours—To Have Laid So Costly a Sacrifice On The Altar of Freedom."

HONOLULU HARBOR has been used for re-provisioning since the earliest visits of sailing vessels, more than 100 years before December 7, 1941.

Dredging has enlarged and deepened the harbor. The dredge deposits on the coral reef have created Sand Island. A drawbridge connects the island with shore which provides the harbor with two entrances. The future plans for Sand Island will keep this harbor in the world shipping picture.

The SS LURLINE departed for California on December 5, 1941. The 600 gay passengers, prepared for a relaxing sea voyage, had a hectic crossing instead. The ship was blacked out, passengers were put on submarine watches, and the full speed ahead zig-zag course taken put them in San Francisco December 10. Radio silence also led to days of apprehension for the passengers and crew.

ALOHA TOWER, completed in 1926, is Hawaii's outstanding landmark and symbol of friendliness and goodwill. At that time, it was the tallest building in Hawaii, but is now dwarfed by many high rise buildings.

Port Authority uses the top floor to control traffic in and out of the harbor, dispatching licensed pilots to take the larger vessels through the harbor channel.

The Dutch liner JAGERSFOUTEIN entered Honolulu Harbor at 9:00 a.m. on December 7th. When bombs began to fall around them the Dutch crew uncovered their guns and fired back. Holland was already at war and became the first allies to join our fight.

From December 7, 1941, to October, 1944, Hawaii was under Martial Law headed by a Military Governor. Honolulu Harbor and all facilities were under direct military control through that period.

7.

KAMEHAMEHA SCHOOLS were
built on the slopes of the mountain, above the city, in 1887. Bernice Pauahi Bishop founded the schools and, by her will, trust funds support and maintain them.

Bernice Pauahi, a direct descendant in the Kamehameha line, married Charles Bishop of New York in 1850, and later declined to become ruler of Hawaii. She retained her devotion to her people and provided in her estate for a girls school and a boys school to provide education for children of Hawaiian ancestry.

Through the years the executors of the estate have had to define this ancestry to match the changes caused by intermarriage.

During the Pearl Harbor attack of December 7th a wall of one of the buildings was damaged by a shell explosion. In 1942 the entire Girls School was set up as a 750 bed Army Hospital.

TRIPLER U.S. ARMY HOSPITAL

was started in 1944. Because of the scarcity of materials and manpower the 14 story building was only partially completed at the end of the war.

The present site was chosen because space did not permit such a large building at Fort Shafter where the old Tripler General Hospital was located. The Shafter building was the Army's main hospital in Hawaii and was used throughout the war with its capacity increased by use of nearby schools.

The new Tripler was opened in 1948 and has since handled hospital cases for all branches of the service. During the war in Korea it was a welcomed facility in the Pacific and used to capacity. Peacetime accommodations are about 1,500 beds, which can be raised to 2,000 beds in an emergency.

HONOLULU INTERNATIONAL AIRPORT

is located adjacent to Hickam Air Force Base. It is one of the 10 busiest airports in the world. The tower handles an average of one plane every three minutes. Its runways and tower facilities are used by both commercial and military planes.

The new modern airport was opened in 1962 with the terminal building dedicated as the John Rodgers Terminal Building. Before commercial overseas flights the airport was a small landing strip and a few hangars known as John Rodgers Field.

A few private planes and instruction flights were out early on Sunday morning December 7, 1941, and an inter-island flight to Maui was scheduled to take off at 8:00 a.m. Chaos developed just before that hour when Japanese attack planes began to strafe the airport, killing and wounding some of the civilians. The Maui flight passengers were unloaded without being harmed. The small planes in the air all managed to get back even though some were attacked and damaged by bullets.

HISTORY OF PEARL HARBOR

Legends of ancient Hawaii tell of waters called Puuloa, which was the home of the beneficent Shark Goddess Kaahupahau. Her sharks were man's protectors against many evil spirits and also against the other "man-eating sharks." Therefore, these waters were sacred and had many kapus.

The legends, when first recorded in the 19th Century, refer to Ewa as the first area populated on Oahu by the immigrant polynesians. One Ewa king, Chief Keaunui, is credited with deepening the entrance of the harbor to 15 feet in about the year 1650. During those years and into the 20th Century numerous fish ponds and fish traps were in the entrance and in the many lochs of that body of water. Most were maintained for royal use only.

As early as 1796 European visitors recorded that those waters produced oysters which were used for food, and that pearls were frequently found in them. The pearls were milk white, spherical, and of exquisite luster. By 1810 the king had found the trading value of the pearls and kept them under royal control.

In 1810 the river leading into the bay was referred to as Wymumme, and in 1819 as Wy Momi, which translated to English is Pearl River. (The difference in spelling is that of the person recording the spoken word.) Again in 1836 it is recorded that the small pearl oyster was quite abundant and common on the table. From about that time on, the large area of water at the mouth of the river was called Pearl Harbor.

For generations the land surrounding Pearl Harbor was subject to natural erosion and the attrition of "civilization" which allowed much of the harbor to be filled with mud. The oysters could not survive in the mud and were nearly extinct by the late 19th Century.

A visitor from the United States noted in 1840 that there was a depth of 15 feet over the coral bar at the harbor entrance. He suggested to the U.S. Government that they attempt an agreement with the Hawaiian king for the use of the harbor for U.S. ships. This was not acted upon until 1873 and not agreed upon until 1898. Then the actual work of deepening and widening the channel wasn't started until 1901, at which time a coaling station for the fueling of ships was erected just inside the entrance.

THREE HUNDRED FIFTY-THREE JAPANESE PLANES took off from the flight decks of 6 Japanese carriers on the morning of December 7, 1941; 183 at 6:00 a.m. and a second wave of 170 followed at 7:15. Pearl Harbor was the objective of their lethal attack.

The carriers were in a 33 ship task force which moved without detection to 200 miles north of Oahu.

As the planes approached the island they split into three groups. Some dove on Pearl Harbor from the west, strafing the Marine Airfield at Ewa, others from the north hitting Schofield Barracks and Wheeler Field as they came in low towards their main target, and the rest zoomed in from the east past Diamond Head.

At 5 minutes to 8:00 o'clock they converged on Pearl Harbor and by 1:00 p.m. all but 29 were back aboard their carriers.

The Task Force immediately left the area on a direct route to Japan. All but one destroyer of the 33 ships were sunk before the end of the war.

USS CONDOR was on routine minesweeping patrol duty offshore the island of Oahu in the early morning of December 7, 1941.

At about 3:45 a.m. men of her crew spotted a submarine in the restricted waters near the entrance to Pearl Harbor. CONDOR'S skipper signalled to the Destroyer WARD, which was also on patrol and nearby, giving the CONDOR'S position and what they had seen.

As the CONDOR was only equipped for minesweeping, and the WARD was armed with guns and depth charges, they proceeded into Pearl Harbor as their patrol duty time was over.

The anti-submarine nets in the channel had been opened for the CONDOR as she was scheduled to come in at that hour.

13.

USS WARD responded to the message from the CONDOR by speeding to the area named but could not locate the submarine. Both the CONDOR and the WARD considered the idea that one of our own submarines might be in the restricted area by error. The WARD went to battle stations anyway but found nothing.

In the daylight, at about 7:00 o'clock, the WARD sighted a submarine and again went to action stations. They sank that midget Japanese submarine near the Pearl Harbor Channel entrance. The commanding officer of the WARD sent this terse message to the commandant of the 14th Naval District in Pearl Harbor,

"We have attacked, fired upon, and dropped
   depth charges upon a submarine operating
   in defensive sea area."

Neither the text nor the implications of this message were distributed to the fleet in time to warn them of the impending enemy attack.

The destroyer WARD is officially recognized for having fired the first shot of World War II.

Three years later to the day, December 7, 1944, the WARD was sunk at Ormac Bay in the Philippines after a Kamikaze suicide plane crashed on her.

FIVE MIDGET JAPANESE SUB-MARINES,

transported from Japan to Hawaii on the tops of five large Japanese "I" Class subs, took part in the December 7, 1941 attack. The midgets, designed in Germany and built in Japan, varied between 40 and 50 feet in length and used a two man crew. They could fire two torpedoes and also had an explosive charge in the bow for suicidal ramming.

One sub couldn't steer properly and finally beached on the Windward side of Oahu. The skipper was the first Japanese prisoner-of-war and all the other crews were killed in their vessels.

Two of the subs penetrated Pearl Harbor through the open submarine nets an hour or so before the air attack, but did no damage. One of them was sunk by the destroyer MONAGHAN and the other by gunfire from various ships.

The other two were sunk just outside of Pearl Harbor: one by the WARD just before 7:00 a.m. and the other by the light cruiser ST. LOUIS at about 9:45 a.m.

15.

TWELVE B-17 BOMBERS from California arrived over Oahu during the December 7th air raid on Pearl Harbor. They had been unarmed to lighten their loads. Staff Sergeant Lee Embree opened a hatch as Zeros approached, swung out his large aerial camera and recorded the only U.S. aerial pictures of the attack. Enemy pilots apparently thought the camera was a gun and avoided the plane. (This picture taken over the wing of the B-17 shows "Val" dive bombers.)

The other bombers were attacked, but all managed to land; eight at Hickam Field, two at Haleiwa Field, one at Bellows Field, and one on the Kahuku Golf Course.

At Point Kahuku an Army radar operator picked up the Japanese mass of planes about 7:00 a.m. He reported this to his headquarters but the B-17 flight had been widely publicized and it was assumed they were on the radar screen. If the approaching planes had been considered as non-friendly there could have been an alert 50 minutes before the attack.

16.

HICKAM ARMY AIR FIELD had

more than the usual Sunday activities early that day of December 7th as many officers and men were on hand for the arrival of the B-17 flight from California. The Japanese arrived first, bombing and strafing Hickam Field at the same time as they hit Pearl Harbor.

The attack was relentless and set fire to barracks, hangars and planes. The Army bombers that were grouped together along the runway as an anti-sabotage measure were put out of action. The smouldering wreckage of the Japanese destruction was thorough and Hickam Field was out of the fight for that day.

Wheeler Field, 12 miles away, was also bombed and strafed but managed to get some fighter planes up. Other planes took off from Haleiwa Field which was not attacked.

Oahu was home base for about 390 military planes: only 38 were able to get into the air; 10 of them were shot down.

PEARL HARBOR CHANNEL had been protected since 1909 by Fort Kamehameha named after the great Hawaiian warrior and king. That Coast Artillery fort and later Fort Weaver and Fort Barrette covered both sides of the channel with 12 inch mortars and 16 inch naval guns converted to coast artillery use.

That defense was of no protection during the air attack on December 7, 1941. The guns were melted down for scrap in the early days of the war.

The channel's only other defense was the two submarine nets that were stretched across at different points. The defense proved vulnerable as two midget subs followed our ships in while the nets were open.

During the war Fort Kamehameha was used as a clearance center with many thousands of men leaving there for battle and later many for furloughs, rotation, and discharge. The Forts are no longer active.

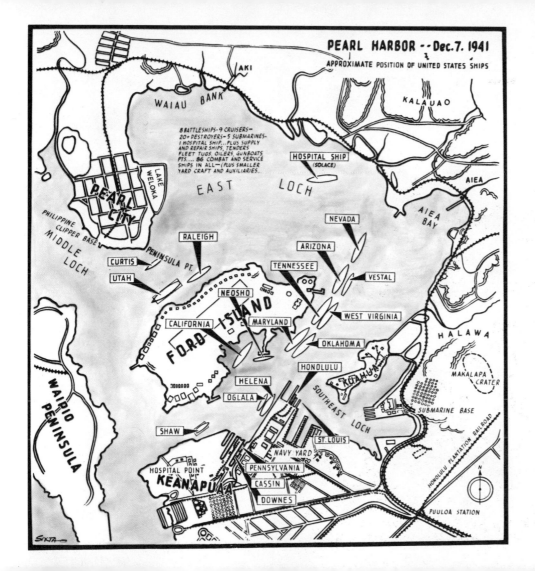

PEARL HARBOR -- Dec. 7. 1941
APPROXIMATE POSITION OF UNITED STATES SHIPS

PEARL HARBOR has 8.5 square miles of water area and there are about 12 miles of docking facilities. The main body of water is joined by smaller areas called lochs and bays.

The present development of the harbor occurred in various stages. In 1902 the channel was dredged to a depth of 35 feet but it wasn't until 1908 that the facilities inside were expanded, as they were again in 1919, 1922, and a great deal more about 1941.

Ford Island is in the center of the main body of water and was the site of the Naval Air Station on December 7th. Both sides of Ford Island were lined with mooring quays and the ones on the southeast side made up a group known as "Battleship Row." At that time, quays were used exclusively by the largest ships because it was difficult to moor them in the smaller docking areas.

19.

PEARL HARBOR NAVAL HOSPITAL

was a small facility on the morning of December 7, 1941. There was a recorded total of 3,478 casualties in the area near the hospital and more than 2,000 needed first aid, medical care, or hospitalization. Teams of doctors, nurses, and aids worked at the Naval Hospital 24 hours a day for 10 days following the attack.

Not only was the Naval Hospital overburdened but the hospitals throughout the city of Honolulu were filled to overflowing. Four school buildings were converted into temporary hospitals because of the need.

Civilian help from doctors, nurses, civilian defense teams, blood banks, and blood donors were immediately available because of a well organized Civilian Defense program. The project was initiated and well formulated in the months prior to the attack and saved many lives.

20.

USS NEVADA was the only battleship to get underway during the air attack on December 7, 1941. One Japanese torpedo hit in the forward section but even with that damage the crew hastily cut her lines as she left the mooring quays. The intention of the commanding officer was to put to sea as ordered. Enemy flyers diverted from other targets and dive-bombed.

As the NEVADA passed abeam of the southwestern point of Ford Island the water around the ship erupted in huge geysers from the dive-bomb drops. She emerged from the spray with her superstructure on fire and her hull a series of gaping holes but she was still under way. So as not to risk sinking and blocking the channel she was ordered to beach herself and deliberately went aground.

In the shallow water and on the hard sand bottom of what is now called Nevada Point, repairs and salvage work went rapidly.

21.

FORD ISLAND NAVAL AIR STATION

and Hickam Field were bombed and strafed simultaneously on December 7, 1941. To prevent counter attacks the Japanese hit the air bases on the island first. The Naval Air Station at Kaneohe, Wheeler and Bellows Army Air Fields and the Marine Air base at Ewa were all attacked at nearly the same time.

Because of the war in Europe the United States had become extremely sabotage conscious. Directives had gone to all branches of the Armed Services to take precautions against possible sabotage. In carrying out those orders planes were taken from hangars and placed in groups along runways. Being out in the open aided the guards watching for saboteurs.

The groups of planes made easy targets for attacking enemy pilots. Ford Island had only three planes able to fly but the men fought their attackers from the ground with machine guns. All the air bases responded with similar action.

22.

USS CURTISS (lower left) sounded General Quarters at 7:55 a.m. just after Ford Island was hit by the first bomb on December 7, 1941. She commenced firing at attacking aircraft and prepared to get underway. At 8:06 a.m. the firing was diverted to an enemy sub off her starboard quarter but the firing ceased as the destroyer MONAGHAN steamed down on the sub.

The CURTISS shot down three planes but didn't leave her mooring because one damaged plane crashed into her setting fires.

Along the northwest side of Ford Island (right to left) are the TANGIER, UTAH, RALEIGH, and DETROIT.

The TANGIER's anti-aircraft firing started at 8:00 a.m. Just after that time its bow guns were fired at the midget sub, but like the CURTISS ceased firing as the MONAGHAN approached. The undamaged TANGIER had four bombs miss her by a few feet.

The picture shown was taken by an attacking Japanese pilot before 8:00 o'clock. The UTAH had already been hit.

23.

USS MONAGHAN was a ready duty destroyer on the morning of December 7, 1941. At 7:51 a.m. she was ordered to get underway immediately and join the destroyer WARD off the entrance to Pearl Harbor. Moving out of East Loch she passed between the CURTISS and the TANGIER as both were firing at the midget sub which had surfaced.

The MONAGHAN put on flank speed, rammed the sub and dropped two depth charges as her bow glanced off of it. That ended the brief career of the sub. The MONAGHAN proceeded out of the harbor to join other ships in the search for the Japanese fleet.

The MONAGHAN earned 12 battle stars and survived many engagements without serious damage. On December 17, 1944, the MONAGHAN capsized in a typhoon near the Philippines. The storm with winds of 110 knots accomplished what the enemy had been unable to do. Only six men of the entire crew survived.

USS UTAH was one of the first ships hit that Sunday of December 7th. She took two torpedoes within five minutes of the beginning of the attack and listed so rapidly the senior officer aboard ordered "abandon ship." No one finished hoisting the flag that was to be raised at 8:00 a.m. By 8:12 the UTAH was bottom up, a total loss.

Four hundred sixty-one men survived the sinking of the UTAH. Fifty-eight perished by the strafing attacks, or were trapped inside the ship. One man was saved by cutting through the bottom.

The UTAH was built as Battleship #31 and during World War I was a Flagship in the Atlantic. In 1931 she was converted to a mobile target vessel with her heavy guns removed and decks of heavy timbers and cement constructed as protection against the practice bombs dropped on her. From 1935 on, UTAH was also designated and staffed as an anti-aircraft training ship but did not have time to use these powerful batteries that morning. She was declared "out of commission" in 1944 when salvage work was abandoned. Being moored in "Aircraft Carrier Row" made her a target for very heavy attacks.

USS RALEIGH was moored just ahead of the UTAH on the northeast side of Ford Island on December 7, 1941. (The capsized UTAH is in background.)

In the first wave of attackers a torpedo hit the RALEIGH on the port side causing a list to such a degree that it appeared she might capsize. Within minutes of the attack her anti-aircraft batteries were firing though the attack of a dive bomber was unavoidable. The ship was strafed and the deck hit with an armor-piercing shell that went through the ship and exploded in the mud under her. As she fought to survive the gunners assisted in the destruction of five planes, blowing the tail off one as it passed astern. By some miracle none of her men was dead and only a few wounded.

The other part of the fight was to keep afloat. The RALEIGH was soon repaired and then went on to fight the enemy.

USS DETROIT was moored just ahead of her sister cruiser the RALEIGH when Pearl Harbor was attacked, December 7th.

The same wave of torpedo planes that hit the RALEIGH and the UTAH sent one torpedo at the DETROIT which skimmed by her and detonated against Ford Island. The DETROIT gun crews got in some hits on enemy planes. However, it was so close to the RALEIGH, and with both ships firing at will, which guns scored was difficult to determine.

The DETROIT was not damaged during the attack. She joined two other cruisers ST. LOUIS and PHOENIX, the destroyers WARD, HELM, MONAGHAN, BLUE, TUCKER, BAGLEY, DALE HENLEY, PHELPS, and other ships in the fruitless search for the Japanese forces.

The DETROIT earned six battle stars. After Pearl Harbor she participated in the Aleutian patrols and occupation of Attu, the attacks on the Kurile Islands, the Iwo Jima and Okinawa assaults and occupations, and the Third Fleet operations against Japan.

USS SOLACE, a hospital ship, was moored in East Loch the morning of December 7, 1941. Her status as a hospital ship was plainly evident: hull painted white, large red crosses on both sides and topside. Japanese flyers did not bomb the SOLACE.

That was fortunate because of the limited facilities at the Pearl Harbor Naval Hospital as well as throughout the city. The medical supplies, equipment and personnel aboard the SOLACE were badly needed.

Launches from the SOLACE were out in the middle of the attack picking up wounded men from the water and returning with them for treatment. The non-medical crew from the SOLACE helped at other ships saving men and equipment.

Moored in East Loch near the SOLACE were destroyer tenders with their groups of destroyers. Some of them went out of the harbor during the attack, and others soon afterwards, to join in the hunt for the attacking forces.

THE FIRST MINUTES OF WAR

are shown in the captured Japanese aerial photograph taken December 7, 1941.

"Battleship Row" along the east side of Ford Island had received it's first torpedoes. Two Japanese planes are in view, one over the NEOSHO and one over Southeast Loch.

The fuel tanks (shown in background) at the Navy's fuel oil storage depot went untouched during the attack. So did the Submarine Base off Southeast Loch (upper right). Early retaliation against the infamous attack was due in large part to the above mentioned facilities escaping damage. The five submarines in the Sub Base during the attack were able to start harrassing the Japanese in the Western Pacific within a few days. Plenty of fuel was available for all ships.

"BATTLESHIP ROW" just after the first torpedoes hit. The explosions made concentric waves in the water. Oil slicks are shown close alongside of the WEST VIRGINIA, OKLAHOMA and CALIFORNIA. More than 2,000 men were killed here in the first 30 minutes of the December 7, 1941, attack.

From left to right are the battleships NEVADA, VESTAL (a repair ship), ARIZONA (inboard), WEST VIRGINIA (outboard), TENNESSEE (inboard), OKLAHOMA (outboard), MARYLAND (inboard), NEOSHO (a tanker), and CALIFORNIA.

The first and very disastrous blows were by 12 torpedo planes that made a low approach from the east over Southeast Loch. Salvaged torpedoes showed that specially contrived wooden fins were fitted to them that made it possible to launch them in shallow water. None of the ships had torpedo nets rigged because they thought the shallow water protected them against torpedoes.

Smoke, in the background, is from the fires started at Hickam Army Air Field following the bombing and strafing of the hangars, planes, and buildings.

USS NEVADA participated in both global wars in the first half of the Twentieth Century. The first oil-burning battleship in the U.S. Navy, the NEVADA was the oldest United States battleship afloat on December 7th. During that attack she went aground. The ship was raised from the mud, refloated, and repaired at Pearl Harbor, and then completely modernized at Bremerton Shipyards.

After a short time in the Aleutians she hurriedly sailed through the Panama Canal for participation in the invasion of France, both on the Normandy Coast and on the Southern Coast. Then she was back in the Pacific for the Iwo Jima, Okinawa, and Japan occupations.

The NEVADA served her country as a "guinea pig" for the Bikini Atom bomb tests in 1946. Surviving the atom tests she was sunk in 1948 by American ships while testing other weapons.

U.S.S. ARIZONA

USS ARIZONA was placed in commission in 1916. For 25 years the U.S. Navy, the people of Arizona, the state for which she was named, and other citizens were proud of the ARIZONA. The mighty dreadnaught of the high seas was prepared to meet any enemy.

The battleship ARIZONA was the third U.S. ship to bear the name. The first ARIZONA was an ironclad side-wheel steamer purchased by the Government in 1863. The second ARIZONA was a frigate launched in 1865. There will be no others named ARIZONA.

The over-all length of the ARIZONA was 608 feet, her beam 97 feet. Her normal displacement was 31,400 tons with a mean draft of 29 feet.

Of her total compliment of Navy and Marine Corps men, some 1550 were on board that fateful morning.

THUNDERING EXPLOSIONS

jolted the mighty ARIZONA as five torpedoes ripped into her portside. In addition, an uncounted number of aerial bombs hit her decks. An armor-piercing shell penetrated the upper decks and continued down into a powder magazine. The explosion that followed knocked out all electrical circuits and all communications. Concussion of the explosion set off the ARIZONA's main forward battery magazine which lay deep in the vessel's hull below gun turrets No. 1 and No. 2. The combined weight of the two turrets was more than 600 tons, including their heavy armor plating and their triple 14 inch guns. The force of that tremendous explosion was so great that it dislodged both of the gun turrets and the conning tower and they all dropped vertically about 20 feet below their normal positions.

The proud ARIZONA went down in the greatest assault ever made on the United States, the treacherous Japanese attack on Pearl Harbor. After many years of service with the fleet in the Pacific her end came with the sudden and enveloping destruction and death of December 7, 1941.

33.

THE ARIZONA was shattered in two and settled to the bottom of the harbor in less than nine minutes. Oil in parts of the hull and on the water burned as a holocaust for hours. The ARIZONA defiantly continued to fly her flag which was hoisted as the attack began.

Two hundred eighty-nine persons survived the terrible explosions and fires although four-fifths of the ship's complement of men were killed. The ARIZONA'S personnel loss was by far the heaviest of all the ships in the harbor.

The bodies of more than 1,100 men are still entombed within the rusting hulk including Rear Admiral Isaac C. Kidd and Captain Franklin Van Valkenburgh, commanding officer of the ARIZONA.

It was decided to let the ARIZONA be a nautical tomb in memory of the men who made the ultimate sacrifice for their country on December 7, 1941.

34.

USS ARIZONA MEMORIAL,

dedicated on Memorial Day 1962, spans the sunken hull of the ARIZONA. It encloses an assembly area large enough for 200 people, a museum and a shrine with the names of those killed.

The flag flies at the top of the mast in memory of all American Servicemen killed on December 7, 1941. The Navy considers the ARIZONA sentimentally in commission. Every morning and evening a Color Guard raises or lowers the flag.

At the foot of the flagpole is a bronze plaque that reads:

DEDICATED
TO THE ETERNAL MEMORY
OF OUR GALLANT SHIPMATES
IN THE USS ARIZONA
WHO GAVE THEIR LIVES IN ACTION
7 DECEMBER 1941
"From today on the USS ARIZONA will again fly our country's flag just as proudly as she did on the morning of 7 December 1941.
I am sure the ARIZONA'S crew will know and appreciate what we are doing." Admiral A. W. Radford, USN
7 March 1950
MAY GOD MAKE HIS FACE
TO SHINE UPON THEM
AND GRANT THEM PEACE

USS WEST VIRGINIA and USS TENNESSEE

were at the quays just south of the ARIZONA on December 7, 1941. The WEST VIRGINIA was outboard of the TENNESSEE and six torpedoes and two bombs left her a flaming wreck. She settled to the bottom with her main deck awash.

After being raised and repaired the "WEEVEE" went back into the war. She spent 223 days in battle actions and took on all comers to the finish.

The TENNESSEE was pinned to the mooring quays until the WEST VIRGINIA was moved. The TENNESSEE'S damage from bombs was not too severe and she was not hit by torpedoes, being protected by the WEST VIRGINIA. A big hazard to the TENNESSEE was burning oil on the water, but the Captain thwarted that by running the propellers full speed ahead for 24 hours, without moving.

The TENNESSEE'S guns fought back throughout the attack. Later she took part in the Iwo Jima and Okinawa campaigns.

36.

USS OKLAHOMA was moored outboard protecting the MARYLAND from torpedoes. The MARYLAND'S damage was the least of any of the eight battleships in the harbor on December 7th. She was in active service in less than three months.

Shortly after the first Japanese bomb exploded on Ford Island the OKLAHOMA was blasted by three torpedoes in rapid succession. There was no time to prevent her capsizing because of the rapid listing. She took two more torpedoes as she capsized. Men were strafed as they climbed over the rolling ship which stopped when the masts hit the mud of the harbor bottom. All of this in less than 20 minutes.

The OKLAHOMA lost 415 men from the total complement of 1,354. Thirty-two men trapped inside were saved by heroic efforts of rescuers who cut through the upturned bottom. The rescue efforts by sailors and civilian workers from the shipyard started during the attack.

USS CALIFORNIA (foreground) has just been hit and is listing slightly. At the stern of the NEOSHO (background) is the upturned bottom of the OKLA-HOMA.

The NEOSHO had just delivered 500,-000 gallons of aviation gasoline to the Ford Island Naval Air Station and had that many more gallons on board. Regardless, her guns opened fire at 8:05 a.m. and are credited with shooting down one enemy plane.

The NEOSHO was the first ship underway. Her captain knew they were blocking the way of the MARYLAND and the OKLAHOMA and while under attack chopped the mooring lines and backed away from the pier. The NEOSHO barely cleared the OKLAHOMA which was just rolling over. She moved to a "safe place."

The NEOSHO was undamaged during the December 7th attack. Only five months later she was sunk in the Coral Sea after being hit by seven bombs and one suicide plane.

GENERAL ALARM was sounded on the CALIFORNIA at 8:00 a.m. the Sunday morning of December 7th. Personnel in the ship's flag communications station watched the first torpedo hit.

At 8:05 a.m. two explosions rocked the CALIFORNIA setting off an ammunition magazine and killing 50 men. The ship took an eight degree list and started to settle. The CALIFORNIA was about to undergo an inspection, and watertight integrity was not at maximum accounting for the immediate flooding.

Bomb hits now started fires, and burning oil in the water made a wall of fire surrounding the ship. "Abandon ship" was ordered. The men immediately started fighting the fires with equipment from Ford Island. Soon "abandon ship" was cancelled and the men returned. Despite valiant efforts to keep her afloat the CALIFORNIA settled into the mud.

The CALIFORNIA was ready for battle in time for the capture of Saipan and Guam. She was active in all the island occupations up the line to Japan.

THE SECOND WAVE of enemy planes met a concentrated screen of anti-aircraft fire as more ships' crews were ready.

Four cruisers were at the piers of the repair yard in Southeast Loch. The NEW ORLEANS and the SAN FRANCISCO were on opposite sides of one pier and the ST. LOUIS and HONOLULU were side by side at the next pier.

The SAN FRANCISCO engines were under repair and her ammunition was ashore for safety. She went undamaged and cleared Pearl Harbor on December 16th.

The NEW ORLEANS was without power and could man only a few guns. She was ready to be underway December 23.

The HONOLULU had hull damage from a bomb that exploded under the pier but fired 7,750 rounds of ammunition. She went on duty January 2.

The ST. LOUIS' guns had to be operated manually but were credited with three probable "kills" during the attack of December 7th. At 9:31 a.m. she was underway and steamed out at 25 knots, the first big ship to reach open water.

USS OGLALA was outboard of the cruiser HELENA alongside "1010" dock. That was where the battleship PENNSYLVANIA normally berthed, and thus they became prime targets. Torpedoes were launched at the two ships by the first wave of attackers on December 7th. One torpedo passed under the OGLALA and exploded against the HELENA. The blast caved in the side of the OGLALA and she started flooding. Two commercial tugs were hailed. Working under constant danger the tugs towed the OGLALA clear so the HELENA could move out.

The OGLALA was secured to the dock, but capsized at 9:45 a.m. She was raised, rebuilt, and supported the fighting ships through the war as a repair ship.

The HELENA went on her own power for overhaul. While in action in the South Pacific she was sunk by Japanese torpedoes off New Georgia on July 5, 1943. Of the 739 men rescued, 165 spent 36 hours in the water and another 8 days on a jungle island before rescue.

THE BATTLESHIP PENNSYL-VANIA

and the destroyers CASSIN and DOWNES were out of the water at Drydock No. 1.

The PENNSYLVANIA was not damaged seriously, and soon was in action. She was Flagship on December 7th, but never again. On August 12, 1945, just two days before the war's end the PENNSYLVANIA was hit by a torpedo at Okinawa, the last major ship damaged in action.

The CASSIN and the DOWNES had raging fires under them from ignited fuel. The drydock was flooded to control the fires. Flooding caused the CASSIN to slip from her keel blocks and fall against the DOWNES. Both were thought to be lost.

The CASSIN was towed to San Francisco and rebuilt. It was her record to earn seven battle stars before the surrender of Japan.

All salvageable machinery and equipment of the DOWNES were shipped to Mare Island, and built into another hull. Her last duty was carrying homeward bound servicemen from Iwo Jima to California.

42.

USS SHAW suffered a devastating bomb hit which came late in the attack on December 7th. The detonation hit forward blowing up all the magazines and tearing off the entire bow. Debris and shells sailed through the air landing all around Pearl Harbor. The destroyer was in Floating Drydock No. 2. After the spectacular explosion the SHAW was reported sunk by Japanese flyers.

Pearl Harbor Shipyard workers fashioned a new wooden bow, and with it the SHAW made a tedious voyage to San Francisco for permanent repairs. In July, 1942, she steamed out of the Golden Gate in her new battle dress. In October, less than one year after being a Pearl Harbor casualty, the ship was in action in the Solomons.

The SHAW was under attack in 11 battle actions winning stars for that number. Battle damage put her in drydock one more time. On V-J Day she was in San Francisco.

USS PHOENIX steamed by the burning ARIZONA on her way to sea. Moored in East Loch near the SOLACE observers on the PHOENIX sighted the rising sun of Japan on the strange planes coming in low over Ford Island. They put these planes under fire in the early minutes of the December 7th attack.

The PHOENIX was one of the ships unharmed during the disaster. Her escape was probably due to the attention enemy airmen paid to the capital ships in nearby "Battleship Row."

During 15 months in the forward fighting areas the cruiser earned 9 battle stars in 20 different actions. She is credited with shooting down eight torpedo or Kamikaze planes attacking her, and sinking a sub that had fired two torpedoes at her.

One enemy bomb burst in the water close aboard the PHOENIX wounding four men and killing one, the only man killed aboard the PHOENIX throughout the war. She well deserved the nickname "LUCKY PHOENIX."

ONE JAPANESE PLANE shot down crashed in Honolulu. Japanese carriers dispatched 353 planes, 29 of them never returned. They were hit by anti-aircraft fire, or shot down in "dog-fights" with Army planes. Enemy planes crashed all over Oahu, in Pearl Harbor, and in the ocean offshore. No serious damage to civilians or their property was reported from the crashes.

Strict blackout regulations and enforcement went into effect the night of December 7. Something more was expected to happen. At 7:14 p.m., as Islanders sat in their dark homes or in dark shelters, police radio announced that Pearl Harbor was being attacked again. There was an extravagant display of fireworks over Pearl Harbor. Six planes from the aircraft carrier ENTERPRISE were coming in to land at Ford Island. Four of the planes were shot down. Sleep that night was scant for adult civilians and military personnel.

CIVILIAN CASUALTIES included three Pearl Harbor employees on their way to their jobs. Sixty-eight were killed, 50 or more were wounded needing hospitalization and more than 200 others less seriously wounded. Most of the casualties were on or near military bases, but others were in Manoa Valley, Downtown Honolulu, the Airport, Ewa, and Waipahu.

The records of a Honolulu utilities office show more than 40 locations where bombs or shells impacted and were investigated. Twenty-five of them caused damage to buildings and persons, 7 caused slight damage, 3 were followed by fires, and 9 had no explosion or damage. Civilian damage on that day has been estimated at $500,000.

The opinion of experts is that most of the damage was a result of anti-aircraft fire from U.S. guns. Strafing near military bases and some bombs were definitely from the attackers, although their general plan obviously was to concentrate on military ships and airfields.

USS NEVADA is shown leaving Pearl Harbor three months after the attack. The Japanese claimed they "destroyed to pieces" many ships that later showed up attacking them.

There were 94 vessels in the harbor at the time of the Japanese attack: 8 battleships, 9 cruisers, 31 destroyers, 5 submarines, and other auxillaries. By the end of the attack, about 9:45 a.m., 18 of them were damaged or sunk and couldn't get under way.

All but 3 of the 18 damaged ships were repaired, and went into action in the weeks and months following the attack. The CASSIN and the DOWNES were rebuilt, and were never stricken from the active list.

Three were total losses. The OKLAHOMA was floated, sold for salvage, and sank at sea while being towed to the West Coast.

The UTAH and the ARIZONA were left at their moorings, and there remain to honor the men who gave their lives in action December 7, 1941.

Sincere appreciation is acknowledged to these individuals for their information or assistance in preparing this book.

Marion P. Goddard, Honolulu; Sara Jean Rice, Honolulu; J. A. Nowell, JO 2, Pearl Harbor; Captain G. T. Curren, USN (Ret); Staff Sergeant Lee Embree, USAF; Grant Chapman; Staff of Colvin's Camera Center, Honolulu; Staff of Bishop Museum Library, Honolulu; Staff of 14th Naval District Office of Public Information, Pearl Harbor; Staff of National Archives, General Services Administration, Washington, D.C.

PHOTO CREDITS